Puss in Boots

A family pantomime

Further titles from LinguaBooks

Drama
Aladdin
Narrowboat Blues

Short stories
In A Strange Land
A Busker on Bow Street
Lost Dreams
The Farmer's Son
The Seasonal Visitor
The Taste of Rain

Fantasy
The Legend of Sidora

Language
Gateway English

Puss in Boots

A family pantomime

by Roy Byrom

LinguaBooks

Roy Byrom has asserted his right under the Copyright, Designs and Patents Act, 1988 to be identified as the author of this work.

ISBN (paperback edition): 978-1911369462

eISBN (digital edition): 978-1911369479

First edition

Editor: Ann Claypole

Copyright © 2021 LinguaBooks

All rights reserved. No part of this publication may be reproduced, stored in a retrieval system or transmitted, in any form or by any means, electronic, mechanical, photocopying, recording or otherwise, without the prior permission of the publishers.

A CIP catalogue record for this book is available from the British Library.

This book is sold subject to the condition that it shall not, by way of trade or otherwise, be lent, resold, hired out or otherwise circulated without the publisher's prior consent in any form of binding or cover other than that in which it is published and without a similar condition including this condition being imposed on the subsequent purchaser.

LinguaBooks
Elsie Whiteley Innovation Centre
Hopwood Lane
Halifax HX1 5ER

www.linguabooks.com

Performance Rights

No performances of this work are permitted without the author's express permission

Production and license enquiries should be addressed to:

LinguaBooks
Elsie Whiteley Innovation Centre
Hopwood Lane, Halifax HX1 5ER
United Kingdom
Tel. 01422 399 554
info@linguabooks.com

A licence issued to perform this pantomime does not include permission to use any incidental music specified in the present work. Licensees are solely responsible for obtaining written permission from the respective copyright owners to use copyrighted music and/or lyrics during the performance of this work. Accordingly, licensees are solely responsible and liable for all music clearances and shall indemnify the copyright owners of this work and their publishers and agents against any costs, expenses, losses and liabilities arising from the use of copyrighted music and/or lyrics by licensees.

Billing and credit requirements

All advertising and publicity material (leaflets, programmes, flyers, posters, etc., including any announcement made via digital or social media) relating to any actual or indented production of this work must include the following billing details, each item of which shall be displayed in a prominent form and position:

Puss in Boots
a family pantomime
by Roy Byrom
in association with LinguaBooks

Foreword

Whilst on the one hand, the story of Puss in Boots is a classic fairy tale incorporating magic, romance, a rise to fame and the quintessential struggle between good and evil, it is also a highly amoral fable, one in which cunning and trickery are seen to succeed, although arguably with the best of intentions and in the spirit of undying loyalty, albeit in a servant-master relationship. But in its panto form, the reworking of this sixteenth-century adventure yarn, transcends the confines of these foibles and becomes more than the sum of its parts. It is, above all, the epitome of live entertainment.

Apart from the eponymous anthropomorphic protagonist famously outwitting a shape-shifting monster, there are a number of features that make Puss in Boots startlingly unique, whilst at the same time, the colourful array of characters and the inevitable progression of the plot line are firmly seated in the British pantomime tradition. And Roy Byrom's new version delightfully embraces all the classic elements of the genre, from song and dance and set pieces to verbal comedy and slapstick in a subtle segue from tradition to originality.

The story of Puss in Boots can be traced back to the tale *Costantino Fortunato* ('Lucky Costantino') by the sixteenth-century Italian author Giovanni Franceso Straparola, who included it in a collection of stories and fairy tales published under the title of *Le piacevoli notti* ('The Pleasant Nights', but more often referred to as 'The Facetious Nights of Straparola') in Venice sometime around 1553. The collection itself was at least in part inspired by Boccaccio's fifteenth-century masterpiece *Decameron*, in turn often tellingly nicknamed 'The Human Comedy.'

The magical legend and its characters have undergone many transformations since then, notably in the form of *Le Maître Chat, ou le Chat Botté* published in 1697 in Paris and translated into English in 1729 by Robert Samber, who thereby gave us the first version of its modern title, 'The Master Cat, or Puss in Boots.' Clearly, it was only a matter of time before this magical story joined the likes of Dick Whittington, Snow White, Robin Hood and Aladdin to become a staple of the British pantomime tradition.

The term 'pantomime' is derived from the Greek *pantomimos*, meaning an 'imitator of all' and indicating an actor or dancer who performed all the roles. In today's pantos, this blending of roles is still in evidence, not embodied by a single performer, but portrayed in an extravagant exotic setting populated with larger than life villains and heros in which cross-dressing, music, comedy and melodrama all play their part. In its modern incarnation, the mere mention of the word 'pantomime' conjures up an unworldly dimension in which, within the strict confines of a defined structure, anything goes.

More than any other type of theatre – or any other form of entertainment at all, for that matter – panto thrives on the participation of a live audience. After all, what noise can be more uplifting than the concerted reverberation of a packed auditorium yelling 'He's behind you!' and responding to 'Oh no, he isn't!' with a defiant 'Oh yes, he is!'?

The result of all these threads coming together is great fun for people of all ages, a theatrical treat that knows no bounds in terms of age and one that, despite the almost feudal historical context, is in its way classless, timeless and universal in its appeal.

Perhaps it is ironic that it is from the centuries-old framework of this topsy-turvy European literary and theatrical tradition rooted in the zaniness of the *Commedia Dell'Arte*, that the modern British panto has created a world in which gender and other boundaries are fleeting and in which anyone can feel at home, an egalitarian environment which can rightly be seen as a celebration of diversity and inclusion.

Maurice Claypole, 2021

Characters

Puss	F	The witting hero
Jack Dumpling	F	The unwitting hero
Princess Annabel	F	What a catch!
Dame Dumpling	M	With dumplings like those, who needs enemies?
Stewart Dumpling	M	The mad scientist
Wilhelm	M	A royal aide de camp
Ivan Itch	M	A smart alec
Hugo Scratchett	M	A not-so-smart alec
Queen Sybil	F	Not to be trifled with
King Basil	M	A trifle royal
The Good Fairy	F	Still trying hard after all these years
Demon Wolf	M	All growl and whiskers
The ogre	M/F	A shape shifting monstrosity

Props

A list of props and sound effects is included at the back of the book.

Scenaria

PROLOGUE

ACT ONE

Scene One   The village square

Scene Two   The Dumpling coffee trolley

Scene Three A forest glade

Scene Four A path through the woods

Scene Five The royal throne room

INTERVAL

ACT TWO

Scene One   A forest glade

Scene Two   A path near the palace

Scene Three The ogre's castle

Scene Four Dame Dumpling's boudoir

Scene Five The royal palace ballroom

ACT ONE

PROLOGUE

House curtains open (tabs are closed). DEMON WOLF *enters sinisterly and stays down left, taking a haughty stance.*

DEMON   So here we are again, my 'friends', another pantomime. Another chance for me to do my dirty deeds, defeating the good, and bringing unhappiness and misery to everyone - especially to you *(menaces* AUDIENCE*)* I HATE BOYS AND GIRLS, especially little ones, like you and you, and you! This year, I shall defeat the good and honourable people of this pantomime. You just wait and see.

FAIRY *enters stage right.*

FAIRY   Yes, we shall see, you Demon vile.
I will protect my friends erstwhile
From all your ranting, bilge and bile
And bring this pantomime to a happy ending.

DEMON   Oh yes? This looks like it'll be an easy job for me. Call yourself a fairy? Just look at you! You're no spring chicken. You should be appearing in Last of the Summer Wine, not a ruffty tuffty panto like this one!

FAIRY   Calling names, my evil foe,
Will not daunt me as on I go
I'll match you Demon, blow for blow.
The good you'll never vanquish.

DEMON   Ha Ha Ha! Tis folly to think that your ancient magic will defeat ME!!! And don't expect to get any help from this rabble. You'll all help ME, won't you? OH YES, YOU WILL.

AUDIENCE   OH NO, WE WON'T.

DEMON   OH YES, YOU WILL.

AUDIENCE   OH NO, WE WON'T.

DEMON   QUIET, or I'll turn you all into frogs! Enough of this, I have evil work to do. Just mark my words. Ha Ha Ha!

Menaces AUDIENCE *and exits stage left.*

FAIRY   Thank you, friends, for your support.
             I think I'll need some more rapport
             If lessons to this fiend be taught
             Before the end of the panto...

             I'm here to help, and as fairies go
             I'm not too old for this show.
             Everyone's got to earn some dough.
             So, if help is needed, call for me.
             Bye-eee!

She waves magic wand at curtain and exits.

Tabs open.

ACT ONE
Scene One
The village square

Opening chorus.

Song 1: big production number
CHORUS, DANCERS, IVAN and HUGO

Posed ending, girls cluster in groups. IVAN *pulls* HUGO *to front.*

IVAN *(eyeing the girls and confidentially to* HUGO*)* There, I told you, didn't I? The village is full of pretty young things just waiting for two suave, sophisticated chaps like us to whisk them off their feet.

HUGO *(doubtfully)* Do you think so, Ivan? They do look gorgeous.

IVAN I do think so, Hugo. Just watch this *(*IVAN *moves to dancer.)* Hello, sweetheart, where have you been all my life?

GIRL 1 For your first thirty years, I wasn't even born! *(*CHORUS *laugh.)*

IVAN Huh! *(Undeterred he finds another.)* Ah, you look like the ideal woman, will you marry me?

GIRL 2 No fear, I'm looking for the ideal man!

CHORUS *howl with laughter and run off.*

HUGO *(laughing and mimicking)* "Just watch this," he says! So much for your suave sophistication.

You're a failure. You're not a complete failure, though ... some parts of you are missing.

IVAN	Listen you, I'll have you know I can marry anyone I please.

HUGO	Why don't you then?

IVAN	Because up to now, I haven't pleased anyone!

HUGO	*(fed up)* Oh well, it looks like it's going to be one of those quiet days, like yesterday... and the day before... and the day before that.

STEWART DUMPLING *enters.*

STEW	Well, well, what do we have here? Ivan Itch and Hugo Scratchett. Lock up your daughters quick!

IVAN	Oh look, it's [Halifax's] answer to the Great British Bake Off: Stewart Dumpling.

HUGO	The only man I know who sells cheap parachutes ... no strings attached! *(boom boom from percussion)* That's the sound of two landing! *(*IVAN *and* HUGO *laugh,* STEWART *doesn't)*

STEW	Now, now, let's be neighbourly. What have you two been up to?

HUGO	We're on our way back from the market.

STEW	*(nods at* IVAN*)* You didn't manage to sell him, then? Mind you, I'm not surprised; I haven't seen anything like that since I saw the film 'Ghouls of [Gibbet Street]'. I'll say one thing for your friend though, he's not two-faced.

HUGO   How d' you mean?

STEW   Well, if he was, he'd wear the other one, wouldn't he?

IVAN   I've never been so insulted in all my life.

STEW   You should get out more!

IVAN   Come on Hugo, we don't have to put up with this.

IVAN *and* HUGO *exit.*

STEW   Ooh, do you know, I can't help it, I'm a little devil at times. HELLO, BOYS AND GIRLS. *(little response)* I said, HELLO, BOYS AND GIRLS. *(more response)* That's better. I'm Stewart Dumpling. No, not stew and dumplings, Stewart Dumpling!! I'm Dame Dumpling's son, and I've got a brother called Jack. Our Jack's got a cat, our Jack has! Talks to it ALL the time. I think he's a bit weird. Don't you think that's weird, Missis? Oops, sorry, Sir. He calls his cat 'Puss'... how original! But I've got nobody.

AUDIENCE   Aahh!

STEW   I said I'VE GOT NOBODY!!

AUDIENCE   Aahh!!

STEW   That's better. I say, will YOU be my friends? WILL YOU BE MY FRIENDS? Every time I come on, I'll shout, HELLO, FOLKS and I want you to shout, HELLO, STEW. Will you do that? Super, let's have a practice. HELLO, FOLKS.

AUDIENCE	HELLO, STEW.
STEW	Oh, you can shout louder than that. Let's try again. HELLO, FOLKS.
AUDIENCE	HELLO, STEW.
STEW	I know, let's see who can shout the loudest, the boys or the girls. Who thinks the girls can shout loudest? *(GIRLS reply)* And who thinks the boys can shout the loudest? *(BOYS reply)* Right, this is just for the girls; you shout back 'Hello, Stew'. HELLO, GIRLS.
GIRLS	HELLO, STEW.
STEW	HELLO, BOYS.
BOYS	HELLO, STEW.
STEW	HELLO, GIRLS.
GIRLS	HELLO, STEW.
STEW	HELLO, BOYS.
BOYS	HELLO, STEW.
STEW	HELLO, MUMS AND DADS.
AUDIENCE	Mumble, mumble *(ALL laugh)*
STEW	*(laughing)* They didn't know the words, did they? Well, that's marvellous, don't forget now. See you later, bye. *(exits)*

DAME *enters on skateboard or scooter, screaming, crosses stage, exits the other side (crashes SFX) and staggers back on.*

DAME   Hello, everybody. What a way to travel ... it's given me quite a turn. Ooh, give me a minute to unpack the bags under me eyes. *(pants)* I'm Dame Dumpling and *(looks around confidentially)* I am the star of the show! I know it doesn't say so in the script, but we've got such riff-raff in the cast this year. You just can't get the staff these days.
Anyway, there's a star on my dressing room door. Well, it's not so much of a dressing room as a washroom, and it's not so much of a star as a little sign saying 'Ladies', but you have to take what's going in this business. I have to take what's going, I'll tell you. Thank you!! Just watch your lip.
AND... I nearly didn't make it. I had to go to the doctor's. I've been poorly.

AUDIENCE   Aaahh!

DAME   I've been more poorly than that!

AUDIENCE   AAAHHH!!

DAME   That's better. Yes, *(hitches up her bust; looks round, confidentially)* women's troubles. *(confidentially again, just mouthing this time)* women's troubles. You know what it's like girls, don't you. The doctor examined me all over. Well, he got a surprise, I can tell you. Then he examined me all over again!! Couldn't believe it the first time. Anyway, he said he couldn't find anything wrong with me and it must be the drink. So, I said I'd go back when he was sober!

Now then, have you met my son Stewart yet? Have you? You have? He's a lovely boy! Have you met my other son, Jack ... and his cat? Oh, you will soon! Do you know, we're so poor I just don't know what we are going to do. *(breaks down sobbing, blows hankie to foghorn effect)*

JACK *and* PUSS *(on all fours) enter.*

JACK   Hello, Mother. What's the matter?

DAME   *(jumps, surprised)* Oh nothing, Jack. I've just been telling those nice people out there that we're very poor and we don't know what we're going to do. I think that they were just about to have a whip-round when you came in.

JACK   Oh, Mother, you are incorrigible.

DAME   No, I'm not, I never went to corridge!! I left school at 16, WHICH ISN'T VERY LONG AGO!! Hey, watch it you!!

JACK   I don't think you've much chance of a whip-round from this lot, they're from Yorkshire. *(cheer)* Don't worry, something will come up.

DAME   Something'll come up alright, my indigestion tablets are not working too well!!

JACK   You mark my words, Mother. Something will turn up, I just know it. So, come on, cheer up.

Enter CHORUS, *run to* DAME.

CHORUS   Don't be sad Dame Dumpling, we can cheer you up.

DAME   Is that a cue for a song?

JACK   It certainly is.

**Song 2: ALWAYS LOOK ON THE BRIGHT SIDE OF LIFE
JACK and DAME DUMPLING and CHORUS**

STEW *enters.*

STEW   HELLO, FOLKS.

AUDIENCE)
CHORUS   )   HELLO, STEW.

STEW   Hello, Mother, Jack. Guess who I've just seen heading this way?

JACK   Not Lewis Capaldi?

DAME   Ooh, I hope it is. I love the music from his 'Four Seasons' CD.

STEW   No, it's not. That's Vivaldi! He composed the Four Seasons.

DAME   *(singing)* Oh, what a Night, Late December back in sixty-three!

STEW   And that's the other Four Seasons, Mother! You know all the right tunes, but not necessarily with the right performer! No, it's the royal family. *(STEW and JACK bow, DAME curtsies.)* The King and Queen, HERE in our village.

IVAN and HUGO *quickly enter, followed by* CHORUS.

IVAN Hey, guess who we've just seen heading this way?

JACK It wouldn't be the royal family *(men bow, ladies curtsy)* by any chance would it?

HUGO Gosh, how did you know?

DAME You two are just like the [Courier] ... always late with the news.

Enter QUEEN, KING, PRINCESS *and* WILHELM.

QUEEN *(loudly)* Really Basil, this is just not good enough, breaking a carriage wheel, miles from anywhere.

KING Yes, Sybil, but our horseman will get us another carriage soon so we can be on our way.

QUEEN I do hope you are right this time, Basil, we have much to do today.

KING Yes, my dear. But this is such a lovely place. *(looks round and sees villagers)* Ah, good day to you. *(*ALL *bow and curtsy.)*

ALL Good day, Your Majesty.

KING Do meet Queen Sybil *(*ALL *bow and curtsy.)*

IVAN *(aside)* Blimey, she looks like a right nag bag!

KING And Princess Annabel. *(more bows and curtsies)*

JACK *and* PRINCESS *start to gaze longingly at each other.*

KING	And the Princess's attendant, Wilhelm – Willie for short.
WILL	Absolutely charmed, I'm sure. *(more bows and curtsies)*
QUEEN	*(notices* PRINCESS *showing an interest in* JACK*)* Just how long are we going to have to wait, Basil? *(She pulls* PRINCESS *to her side to break the trance.)* This outing is going drastically wrong.
KING	Yes, my precious. I'm sorry.
WILL	Excuse me, Sire.
KING	Yes, Willie, what is it?
WILL	While we are strolling about, I don't suppose we could pop into [Harvey's] and do a bit of shopping, could we?
KING	I don't see why not; what about you Annabel?
PRINCESS	*(dreamily)* I think that would be a lovely idea.
QUEEN	Come along then; you'd better be quick. I don't want to miss our rescue carriage.
KING	No, Sybil.

QUEEN, KING, WILL *and* PRINCESS *(lingeringly) exit.*

JACK	*(walking towards exit)* Wow, what a beauty!

STEW	D'you mean Willie? *(They sing "Willie won't go home" – The Sweet.)*
JACK	Oh, you are stupid at times, no - I mean that beautiful Princess.
DAME	This is so exciting. I've never been so close to a King and Queen before.
JACK	Well, I think we've had all the excitement we're going to get today. We'd better move on. What a beautiful girl though. I have a feeling this is going to be a lovely day.

Song 3: IT'S A LOVELY DAY TODAY
JACK, DAME, STEW, IVAN, HUGO and CHORUS

JACK and PUSS *exit.*

Tabs close.

END OF SCENE ONE

ACT ONE
Scene Two
The Dumpling coffee trolley

This scene can be played out in front of the curtains for a scene change.

STEW *enters.*

STEW   HELLO, FOLKS.

AUDIENCE   HELLO, STEW.

STEW   Absolutely brilliant! Are you enjoying yourselves?

AUDIENCE   YES.

STEW   What do you think of the show so far?

AUDIENCE   RUBBISH.

STEW   Well, make the most of it, it ain't going to get any better. *(confidentially)* I'm going to let you into a secret... *(looks round to make sure no-one's there)* I'm a bit of an inventor in my spare time. I don't suppose you know that I invented the zip fastener... No, not many people know that... I got knighted you know... I was called Lord of the Flies!
Well, I want to try out my latest invention. Just stay there a minute. Don't go away. *(STEW goes off and brings on the Coffee Machine.)* There... impressed or what? What do you mean, what is it? This is Stewart's Starbucks Special ... the Dumpling Coffee Trolley. All I need now is someone to test it on.

HUGO *enters.*

STEW   Ah, Hugo. What a pleasure to see you.

HUGO   *(suspicious)* My, you've changed your tune. What are you after?

STEW   Nothing my friend. In fact, I would like to give you something. *(aside)* In more ways than one! Allow me to buy you a coffee.

HUGO   There's something fishy going on here.

STEW   *(aside)* There could be!

HUGO   Still, why not? OK, I'll have a coffee. I'll have a tall skinny latte with Mocha and chocolate sprinkles!

STEW *puts money in, sound effects and cup appears.* HUGO *moves forward to get a coffee and is splattered in the face with water.* HUGO *reacts,* STEW *doubles up.* JACK *has entered and sees* HUGO *all wet.*

HUGO   Why you! Just you wait.

JACK   Not another one of your little tricks, Stew?

STEW   Hello, Jack, would you like a coffee?

JACK   OK, I'll have one, thank you. *(aside)* He is simple isn't he; I know how it works now.

STEW   There you are then; it's there. *(stands back smiling)*

JACK   This is going to be easy.

JACK *approaches and crouches alongside hole, as he gets near, hammer smacks him on the head.*

JACK OW! *(staggers, others laugh)*

IVAN *enters and has seen this.*

STEW *(to* JACK*)* Thought it would be easy, did you?

IVAN This looks like good fun.

HUGO We're trying to get coffee out of this infernal machine. It's not easy.

IVAN No? Well, it should be, I've seen how it works.

STEW Alright then, bossy britches, you get the coffee then.

IVAN No problem, as I always say, it's just a matter of position.

IVAN *bends down away from machine and stretches his arm backwards, backing slowly. Hammer lurks ready to pounce as he gets closer and backs off. IVAN makes a lunge backwards and bottom flap opens and smacks him on the backside.* ALL *fall about laughing as he reacts.*

JACK There must be a way to do this, let's think a minute.

DAME *enters.*

DAME What's going on here? It looks like something from Harry Hill's TV Burp!

HUGO	We're trying to get a cup of coffee from this machine.
DAME	Well, that shouldn't be too difficult, should it? Let me have a go.
HUGO	Don't, Dame Dumpling, it squirts water.
JACK	And hits you on the head.
IVAN	And at the other end. *(rubbing his posterior)*
DAME	Oh, it's just a matter of having a plan of attack, you'll see. Right, if we all go for it at the same time, someone will get the coffee.
JACK	Yes, I suppose so. It's worth a try.
DAME	Ready? ... After three. One, two, three.

HUGO, JACK *and* IVAN *rush at the machine and all get clobbered and end up on the floor.* DAME *gets coffee and takes a sip.*

DAME	Ah, that's grand. You see, all you needed was a plan of attack. Cheers, Stew.
STEW	You're welcome.

DAME *exits.*

STEW	I think I'd better make myself scarce. *(to* AUDIENCE*)* See you later, bye.

STEW *hides behind machine.* OTHERS *exit shouting* "After him". STEW *exits pushing machine.* JACK *and* PUSS *enter immediately.*

JACK   I hope that teaches him a lesson. One of these days he might invent something that's useful.

DAME *enters agitated and upset with a letter.*

DAME   Oh, Jack, Jack. I've just had it. It's awful, really awful. I don't know what to do!

JACK   Steady on and calm down, Mother. What have you got that's so awful. Your boil hasn't come back again has it?

DAME   This is no laughing matter Jack. I'm full of constip... er... consternation.

JACK   Come on, out with it.

DAME   I wish I could! *(dramatic pose)* The rent on the cottage is going up... doubling!

JACK   Isn't that in Ireland?

DAME   Oh Jack, why can't you ever be serious?

JACK   I'm sorry, Mother, but it doesn't seem that serious. You don't pay the rent now. So, it doesn't matter much if you don't pay double, does it?

DAME   But that's just it. They want the arrears paying in the next 10 days. Where can I get the money? I've tried bingo, the pools, the lottery, and the scratch cards. It's no use, we're ruined.

JACK   Now, now, Mother. Something will turn up. You are the nicest and kindest person I know. We will find some way to pay the rent.

Song 4: PUT ON A HAPPY FACE
JACK and DAME with CHORUS and DANCERS

END OF SCENE TWO

ACT ONE
Scene Three
A forest glade

Lights come up on forest glade and DEMON *is front left. Picked up in spot and slowly and deliberately walks forwards.*

DEMON   My plan is beginning to work, unhappiness is descending on these people. Oh, BE QUIET! You ignorant peasants. Don't you realise that you are in the presence of the Master. Once I have attended to my task here, I shall start on you! Dame Dumpling's unhappiness will spread to you all and I shall be victorious. Ha Ha Ha, it is such fun to be evil and horrible. I shall see you again ... very soon. Ha Ha Ha!

He menaces AUDIENCE *and exits left with a flourish.*
FAIRY *enters front right and trips.*

FAIRY   Do not worry my charming friends
No harm will come to you in the end.
The experience of my thirty years
– alright forty, then –
Will lead us through to victory.
Poor Dame Dumpling has had a big shock.
If she doesn't find the money, she'll be in the dock.
She'll have to pawn her very last frock
To try and raise some cash.
They don't deserve a fate so sad
Because people who are good – not bad
Should keep the happiness they had.
It's nearly time for some magic.
But first...

Waves wand and exits front right.

KING, PRINCESS *and* WILL *enter left.*

KING   It's a shame about Dame Dumpling's cottage. They only have a few days to pay the arrears or they will be evicted. ... It's such a pity we can't do anything to help.

PRINCESS   Well, you and Mother are the landlords; there must be something we could do. She really is a kind lady... and her son is very nice, too. Doesn't Mother understand?

KING   Your mother doesn't understand anything. She went to the Doctor because she kept lying on the floor under the bed; he thought she was a little potty! He took me to one side and said he didn't like the look of her. I told him to be thankful he hadn't had to look at her for twenty years like I had.

QUEEN   *(from offstage)* BASIL!

WILL   There's the Queen now, Sire.

KING   Yes Willie. Is there anywhere I can hide?

QUEEN   *(still offstage)* BASIL!

PRINCESS   Mother is heading this way, Father.

KING   *(agitated)* Oh dear! *(to* AUDIENCE*)* She's a nasty spiteful woman, but she's very fair.

PRINCESS   How do you mean, Father?

KING   She's nasty and spiteful to everyone!

QUEEN *enters.*

QUEEN   BASIL! Ah there you are! I've been looking for you everywhere.

KING   Well, here I am.

QUEEN   You're here, but not necessarily well.

PRINCESS   Mother, is there nothing we can do about Dame Dumpling?

QUEEN   Nothing at all, my dear. People must pay their rent.

PRINCESS   But she really is a nice, kind old lady. You can't just turn her out.

QUEEN   You're quite right, my dear. She has seven days in which to pay the arrears. If we let off all the people from paying their rents ... the Royal Mint would have a hole in it.

KING   I must admit we should treat everyone the same.

PRINCESS   Yes, I suppose so.

QUEEN   Come along then Basil, we have papers to prepare.

KING   Yes, Sybil, I had better help you, you know you are not good with paperwork.

Song 5: ANYTHING YOU CAN DO
KING and QUEEN

KING *shrugs shoulders disconsolately as he exits following* QUEEN.

PRINCESS   Oh dear... still we mustn't be sad. Let's hope something turns up. I feel like doing something exciting today, Willie, to cheer me up. Have you got any ideas?

WILL   Not really, Your Highness. I do hope you are not planning anything dangerous.

PRINCESS   No, not dangerous, Willie, but I'm bored being stuck in the palace all the time. It's very tedious at times.

WILL   I know what you mean. How would you like to take a stroll into the village? Remember when the carriage broke down and we had to send for the AA?

PRINCESS   How did you know he was from the AA?

WILL   Well, he came up and said, "Ay Ay, what's up now!" Anyway, we met some nice people down there.

PRINCESS   *(dreamily)* Yes, we did, didn't we. *(pauses)* I think I might have an idea.

WILL   Now, what are you up to, Your Highness? You've got that look on your face that usually means you're up to mischief.

PRINCESS   Oh, don't worry, Willie. I think this is going to turn out to be quite an unusual day.

Song 6: IT'S A MOST UNUSUAL DAY
PRINCESS and WILL with CHORUS and DANCERS

CHORUS *exit.*

PRINCESS   I've had a wonderful idea, Willie.

WILL   Yes, I thought you would have, Your Highness. *(takes a pill)*

PRINCESS   Let's go down to the village again. I think we should try to help Dame Dumpling with the rent somehow. If we go in ordinary clothes, they will think that we are simply villagers strolling around.

WILL   I'm not sure... I'm definitely not sure I like the sound of this. If the Queen finds out, we will be in hot water.

PRINCESS   But the Queen won't find out, will she? *(moves to* WILL*)* Will she, Willie?

WILL   No, I suppose not.

PRINCESS   Come on, let's be quick, I can't wait *(starts to exit)*

WILL   *(following* PRINCESS*)* Ooh, my headache is starting already.

PRINCESS *and* WILL *exit.*
JACK *and* PUSS *(on all fours) enter.*

JACK   Well, Puss, we have only a few more days to find the money to pay the rent arrears or we will be homeless. I must think of something.

FAIRY *enters,* JACK *and* PUSS *freeze.*

FAIRY   Oh dear!
Our hero, Jack is feeling blue.
He's got to figure out what to do.
But here's yours truly, right on cue
To help him with his problem.

I'll have to think of something drastic
To avoid the outcome being tragic.
Methinks we need some fairy magic.
Get ready, Puss, here goes.

FX as FAIRY *casts her magic spell.*
FAIRY *exits.*

JACK   *(unfreezes and continues)* If only we could do what the government do. They cut all the benefits, and just print all the money they need. Oh, how can people be so heartless? *(slumps down dejected)*

PUSS   Master, do not be disheartened. *(*JACK *looks round)* If you do as I say, I will ensure that your life soon changes for the better.

JACK   *(stands)* Who is it? Show yourself. *(to* AUDIENCE*)* Who is speaking? Is it a ghost? Do you know who it is, boys and girls?

AUDIENCE *reply,* JACK *looks bemused.*

PUSS   *(moves to* JACK*)* It is I, Master.

JACK   But you are talking. Cats cannot talk.

PUSS	Normally, we can't. But when good people are in trouble and unhappy all sorts of strange things can happen. I have decided that it is time for me to do something to help.
JACK	I can hardly believe my eyes... or my ears. Am I dreaming, boys and girls?
AUDIENCE	NO!!
PUSS	No, you are not dreaming, Master. You've heard of magic, haven't you? Fairy magic?
JACK	Well, yes, I've heard of it, but I have not really believed in it.
PUSS	*(standing up)* Now you can believe in it. When people are kind and good and think only of others, they make their own kind of magic. I can not only talk, I can think and I can walk. I also know how you can become rich and successful and find lasting happiness.
JACK	Wow!! What do you want me to do?
PUSS	First we need a sack of bran, a box and a smart pair of red leather boots. From now on, I intend to be known as PUSS IN BOOTS. Will you get those things for me, Master, please?
JACK	Yes, of course. *(puzzled)* I am sure I'll wake up soon.

JACK *looks at* PUSS *and exits, scratching his head.*

**Dance 7: CATS music only
dance with PUSS and DANCERS in cat costumes**

End of dance, JACK *returns with box, bran and boots.*

JACK Here we are, Puss. Is this all you need?

PUSS Yes, thank you, Master. What a handsome pair of boots. *(puts on boots with help from* JACK*)* Now I have to get on and work quickly. You must be tired, lie down and rest.

JACK That's a good idea, I feel quite drowsy.

JACK *lies down and falls asleep.* PUSS *sets trap with box and bran, catches rabbit and exits.*

PRINCESS *and* WILL *enter in plain clothes.* JACK *stays sleeping.*

PRINCESS There, I told you we'd have a lovely time when people didn't recognise us. I've seen things today that I'd never dreamed of. People always act strangely and won't talk when they know I am a Princess.

WILL Quite so, Your Highness, but you are a Princess. One day you will meet and marry a rich Prince and later you too can be a Queen. *(pause, looking at* AUDIENCE*)*

PRINCESS Yes, I know, Willie. But before then I want to have a little fun and excitement.

WILL But I am responsible for your safety, and if anything happens…

PRINCESS Nothing will happen, Willie. You worry too much. *(laughs)*

WILL	That's as maybe, but I'd quite like to keep my head and body joined together thank you.
PRINCESS	Oh, you are a silly billy, Willie. This is fun. *(spins round and sees* JACK*)* Ooh, look... there's someone here. *(moves up to* JACK*)* What a handsome young man. He looks familiar... I think I've seen him before. It must have been when we were here last time. Yes... I remember...
WILL	He looks a bit tatty, though.
PRINCESS	But very handsome none-the-less. Willie... will you go and get the carriage and horses ready for our return to the palace? I will be along shortly.
WILL	But, Your Highness...
PRINCESS	*(firmly)* Thank you, Willie!
WILL	Very well, Your Highness.

WILL *bows and exits.*

FAIRY *enters and waves her wand. Lights dim and there is a dream sequence.*

Song 8: OUT OF MY DREAMS music only
JACK and PRINCESS dance

JACK *returns to sleeping position.* PRINCESS *lingers, exits slowly. Lights fade as she exits, and* JACK *exits in dark.*

Dim light and green spot front left.
DEMON *enters left and menaces* AUDIENCE.

DEMON   Oh, belt up! If you are not quiet in an instant, I will make all the interval ice creams melt... and all the tea bags burst. That's better. I am not a happy Demon, all my plans are going wrong. That apology of a fairy has had too much success so far... *(dramatic)* BUT... she will not have everything her way. Now it is my turn to do my meddling and make everyone unhappy again. AND THERE WILL BE NOTHING YOU CAN DO TO STOP ME! Ha Ha Ha HA! QUIET, you raucous collection of imbeciles! All I need now is a couple of ignorant half-wits who can be persuaded to perpetrate my evil schemes.

IVAN *and* HUGO *enter.*

DEMON   Ah ha, right on cue ... my evil powers are still intact. Good day, gentlemen.

They notice DEMON *and react.* HUGO *jumps into* IVAN'S *arms.*

HUGO   Aaaaagh ... What on earth is that Ivan?

IVAN   Whatever it is, it's horrible.

HUGO   It wasn't us.

IVAN   It wasn't me, it was him.

HUGO   It wasn't either of us.

IVAN   There's only one thing to do in this kind of situation. RUN FOR IT! *(*IVAN *and* HUGO *turn to run off.)*

DEMON   STOP!

(DEMON makes magic passes. IVAN and HUGO freeze. DEMON snaps his fingers and they unfreeze.)

DEMON	Don't panic, I'm not going to harm you... *(aside)* yet!
HUGO	Thank you.
IVAN	Yes, we are most grateful.
HUGO	Er... who... er are you... er... sir?
DEMON	I am the Demon Wolf... the villain of this piece... the ogre's henchman... and I have come from Hades.
IVAN	That's a long way to travel just for a pantomime. I hope he's not on expenses.
HUGO	He's probably got a bus pass! Anyway, it's not that far, it's just the other side of [Greetland] isn't it?
DEMON	Enough of this drivel. It is my wont to bring poverty and sadness to this place, and so far my schemes have been thwarted.
IVAN	Well, it is <u>my</u> wont to return to my boring little rut of existence, so if you would kindly excuse us...
DEMON	Oh no!
HUGO	No?
DEMON	No!

IVAN	No-ooh?
DEMON	No!
HUGO	Are you quite sure?
DEMON	I want you to help me.
IVAN	To bring poverty to this place?
DEMON	Yes!
HUGO	To bring sadness to this place?
DEMON	Yes!
HUGO) IVAN)	Should we help him boys and girls?
AUDIENCE	NO.
DEMON	OH YES, THEY SHOULD.
AUDIENCE	OH NO, THEY SHOULDN'T.
DEMON	OH YES, THEY SHOULD.
AUDIENCE	OH NO, THEY SHOULDN'T.
DEMON	SILENCE!! or I shall turn you ALL into stone.

HUGO and IVAN *deliberate, turn as if to speak, turn back again to deliberate, turn as if to speak, turn back to deliberate again and then turn.*

IVAN	Alright, we'll help.

DEMON	GOOD, very wise. You will be well rewarded.
IVAN	Probably with a free bus ride to Hades.
DEMON	This is what I want you to do. Jack's cat has a pair of red boots and is now called Puss in Boots.
HUGO	Oh, yes?
DEMON	I want you to steal those boots.
IVAN	Steal the cat's boots?
DEMON	That's right.
HUGO	Well, that shouldn't be too difficult.
DEMON	Very well, I will meet you in Act Two, Scene One to collect the boots.
HUGO	*(to* IVAN*)* I think he's flipped his lid.
IVAN	*(to* HUGO*)* We'd better do what he says, or we will be turned to stone. *(to* DEMON*)* Very well, we'll meet you and bring the boots.
DEMON	*(to* AUDIENCE*)* So much for your help! Ha Ha Ha! Now MY plan is going to work.

DEMON *exits to boos.*

HUGO	Dame Dumpling is not going to like it!
IVAN	Dame Dumpling hasn't got much chance getting it! Come on, we'd better put our thinking heads on.

HUGO *and* IVAN *exit.*
FAIRY *enters, reading the [Yorkshire Post] (big glasses?), doesn't realise where she is. Then fairy effect.*

FAIRY   *(to sound engineer)* A bit early for you, was I? Sorry, boys and girls, I was just scanning the situations vacant for my next assignment. This one says I need singing and dancing skills. I'd better brush up a bit.

Song 9: NOBODY LOVES A FAIRY WHEN SHE'S FORTY
FAIRY
IVAN *and* HUGO *join in second time through in tutus for a fairy dance, and exit.*

FAIRY   Now... where was I? Oh, yes!!

So, the Demon vile has roped in two
Assistants his dirty work to do.
He won't succeed, this day he'll rue
When he tried to tangle with me.

Even now in advancing years
My magic comes to ward off fears
To keep the good from shedding tears
And make the bad disconsolate.

So, worry not my friends out there
The Good Fairy is here, so don't have a care
Although the cupboard may look bare
It's well stocked in most departments.

The cause of good will always win
Over nastiness, upset and sin.
So, keep your hopes up as we wing
Our way back to the story.

FAIRY *waves her wand and exits.*
Curtain

END OF SCENE THREE

ACT ONE
Scene Four
A path through the woods

Curtain set: A path through the woods.
JACK, DAME and STEW enter.

STEW   HELLO, FOLKS.

AUDIENCE   HELLO, STEW.

JACK   But what I'm telling you is true. Puss started talking and walking and is going to sort out all our troubles ... and then I dreamt that I was dancing with the Princess...

STEW   *(feels* JACK'S *forehead)* Yes, I thought so; he's very hot.

DAME   I think you should take things a little bit easier, you have been overdoing it a bit lately.

JACK   I'm fine, really I am. I know it sounds a bit strange...

STEW   A BIT strange?

JACK   Alright then, very strange ... and I knew you wouldn't believe me. Have I ever told you a lie.

STEW   Well, there was that story you told about you and the vicar's daughter which I don't think was entirely (JACK *stands on his toe.)* OW!!

DAME   No, I must admit, you've never told a lie. You ARE serious aren't you?

JACK	Yes, I am. I know it's hard to understand. In fact, I don't understand it ... but the cat is walking and talking and wearing a brand-new pair of red boots. He's decided to call himself 'Puss in Boots' and he's going to make all our dreams come true.
DAME	You seem very sure, Jack. I do hope you're not going to be disappointed.
JACK	I am sure, Mother. You just wait and see.
STEW	Do you think he can make my dreams come true?
JACK	I don't know how good he is on miracles.
STEW	Oh, thanks.
JACK	You're welcome.

PUSS *enters,* DAME *and* STEW *play up, hiding behind* JACK.

PUSS	There is no need to be afraid, I'm not going to hurt you.
DAME	My, you HAVE changed. I hardly recognised you. *(looks* PUSS *up and down)*
JACK	*(smiling)* Now, I suppose you believe me.
DAME	Well, you must admit it is very extraordinary. You are Puss in Boots, I presume?
PUSS	*(bows)* At your service, ma'am.
STEW	Ma'am? He's obviously no judge of character.

DAME	Belt up, I'm talking to this cat here.
STEW	Blimey, it's catching.
PUSS	Master, I have just come to tell you that everything is working very nicely so far. Very soon all your troubles will be over. You are now known as the Marquis of Carabas.
DAME	Oh, Jack, this is wonderful ... so wonderful I think I'm going to cry.
JACK) STEW)	Oh, not again, Mother.

Song 10: EVERYTHING'S COMING UP ROSES
PUSS, JACK, DAME DUMPLING and STEW

END OF SCENE FOUR

ACT ONE
Scene Five
The royal throne room

Curtains open on royal throne room.
IVAN and HUGO already on stage as attendants.

IVAN	I don't know how we ended up here. I told the chap at the Job Centre that we wanted jobs where we didn't have to do much and where we could live off the fat of the land. They were going to send us to the House of Lords!
HUGO	Never mind that, it's time for sentry duty.

Dance 11: tap/march routine
HUGO, IVAN, CHORUS and DANCERS

HUGO	Hey, being here might give us a chance to steal Puss's boots. That cat has been around a lot lately. And the King has been asking a lot of questions about this mysterious Marquis of Carabas.
IVAN	I know. There are a lot of things round here that are most mysterious.
HUGO	Ugh, don't remind me ... that Demon Wolf fellow is the one who's worrying me.
IVAN	That's a point, we still haven't worked out how to get those boots. Come on, we'd better find a plan or else we might end up propping up a motorway bridge somewhere.

IVAN and HUGO exit.

Enter QUEEN, KING, PRINCESS *and* WILL. KING *rapidly paces up and down.*

KING	I just can't understand all this. That cat has been here every day, bringing gifts from the Marquis of Carabas; first a rabbit, then a pheasant, then a wood pigeon, then a duck. *(they duck, swannee whistle)* I wonder when we are going to meet the Marquis. My curiosity is unbearable.

QUEEN	That's not the only thing that's unbearable, Basil!

KING	*(stops)* No, my precious. *(starts again)* He must be a rich landowner from many miles away.

WILL	*(walks alongside KING, just behind, trying to keep up)* He is indeed a strange man, Sire, and he has a strange animal. Never in all my travels have I come across a talking cat. It is just too much to believe. I think we should follow the cat, Your Majesty ... *(KING stops abruptly to listen, WILL continues)* ... perhaps he will lead us to the lands of the Marquis of Carabas.

KING	What a good idea, Willie. *(WILL stops as he notices the King has stopped.)* You surprise me at times.

WILL	Er ... you are gracious, thank you, Sire *(bows)*

PRINCESS	Can I come too, Father? It will be fun to go on a cat chase.

QUEEN	Certainly not, Annabel. It's much too dangerous for you to go charging around the countryside after a cat.

PRINCESS   Oh, please, Mother. It won't be dangerous and I'll be very careful.

QUEEN   I won't hear of it! I'm sure you have plenty of things to do in the palace. Don't you agree Basil?

KING   Well, maybe it wouldn't be too much of a risk if we...

QUEEN   BASIL?

KING   Yes, my precious, perhaps you are right.

QUEEN   Come along then, Annabel, we will leave the men to their activities.

PRINCESS   Oh, very well. Do be careful, Father.

QUEEN *and* PRINCESS *exit.*

KING   Right, Willie, it's you and I, and we'll take those part-time workers, full-time idiots, Hinge and Bracket.

WILL   You mean Itch and Scratchett, Sire.

KING   Huh ... sounds like a flea circus act. Yes, they'll do. It surely won't take a lot of brains to follow a cat back to its owner. Tell Inch and Bucket to get four horses and a coach ready. NOT the best one this time! Then, as soon as the cat leaves, we can follow straight away. Cancel the rest of my appointments for today. You see to it, Willie.

WILL   Yes, Sire.

WILL *exits.*

KING   Maybe now we will get to the bottom of this mystery.

IVAN *and* HUGO *enter.*

IVAN   The horses are ready without, Sire.

KING   Without what?

IVAN   I mean they are outside ready, Your Majesty.

WILL *enters.*

WILL   I have fixed your appointments, Sire. We are all prepared, and our friend Puss in Boots is just arriving at the palace gates.

KING   Excellent! Now, we'll get to the bottom of this. Now, don't forget, we'd better not lose him, or you'll all be for the dungeons. We haven't had anyone locked up in there for ages. Now, positions everyone.

ALL *take up positions.* WILL *by the 'door'.*

WILL   The Puss in Boots, Your Majesty.

PUSS *enters, bringing another gift.*

PUSS   *(crosses to KING)* Good day to you, Your Majesty. *(bows)* Here is another gift from my master, the Marquis of Carabas; a succulent grouse for your table with his compliments.

KING   Give your master my thanks, he is most kind. But why are you not able to tell us where he is?

PUSS	All will be revealed in time, Your Majesty. Please forgive our secrecy. My master is just as keen to meet you as you are to meet him. He has recently bought a castle and lands adjacent to your kingdom and will soon be inviting you to a dinner and ball in your honour.
KING	That is very gracious of your master. I will look forward to receiving his invitation. While you are here, would you like to visit my table and have a tasty meal of er ... fish ... or ... er Whiskas?
PUSS	You are very kind, Your Majesty, but I must return to my master. We have many preparations yet to make. I am most grateful, but if Your Majesty would excuse me.

PUSS *bows and exits.*

KING	The horses, to the horses before the cat gets too far away. Arch and Sprocket, where are those horses?
HUGO	This way, Sire.
KING	Well, come on then, we have no time to lose, out of my way.

KING *falls over* HUGO, *others rush to help,* ALL *fall over.*

HUGO	I'm extremely sorry, Your Majesty. *(dusts him down)*

Plenty of business getting in each other's way.

KING	Why am I surrounded by idiots? Come on. *(stops and beckons)* After that cat! *(exits)*
HUGO	*(stops and beckons)* After that cat! *(exits)*
IVAN	*(stops and beckons)* After that cat! *(exits)*
WILL	*(stops and beckons, there's no-one there)* After that cat. Hi Ho Silver, away! *(exits)*

Optional chase scene, possibly with strobe, possibly with two cat costumes? Eventually, ALL *exit.*

PUSS *strolls in and walks across.*

PUSS	That is just what I wanted; my plan is working purr-fectly. Me-ow.

PUSS exits.

Curtains close.

END OF ACT ONE

INTERVAL

ACT TWO

ACT TWO
Scene One
A forest glade

Barrel set on stage.
Curtains open.

Dance 12: TALK TO THE ANIMALS music only
speciality 'animal' routine
DANCERS

After dance, ALL exit.
PUSS enters following chase from Act One.

PUSS   HELLO, BOYS AND GIRLS.

AUDIENCE   HELLO, PUSS.

PUSS   Come on, you can do better than that. HELLO, BOYS AND GIRLS.

AUDIENCE   HELLO, PUSS.

PUSS   That's better. We've got them at it now, haven't we? They all think that they're following me without me knowing. They must think that cats are simple. They don't realise they've fallen right into my trap. Now, I think we'll have a little fun. Do you want to have some fun?

AUDIENCE   YES.

PUSS   Brilliant! Well, the King and all the King's men will be along any minute. I am going to hide behind here and when I come out I want you to shout 'Puss is behind you'. Will you do that for me? WILL YOU DO THAT FOR ME? Let's have a practice. *(usual business)* Now, don't forget, oops better go. Here they come.

PUSS *hides.*
Plenty of noise as KING, WILL, IVAN *and* HUGO *come dashing in.*

WILL　　　　I'm absolutely positive the cat came this way. Ooh, look! I can see little boot prints in the mud.

HUGO　　　Are they RED boot prints?

KING　　　　You oaf! You can't see what colour they are, they're just little prints. Do you know, if you had half a brain, you'd be dangerous.

IVAN　　　　*(dry aside)* If he did have half a brain, he would have got the part of King!!!

KING　　　　*(glowers)* I don't think we are far behind him, and I'm sure he doesn't know we are following him. He's going to lead us straight to the Marquis of Carabas.

PUSS *pops out a couple of times, causes confusion, then runs off, round across back followed by* ALL *to exit.*
JACK *wanders in and shortly afterwards* PUSS *enters.*

PUSS　　　　Ah, there you are, Master. Everything is working out very nicely. You wouldn't believe the lengths people are going to to meet you.

JACK　　　　I'm very flattered.

PUSS　　　　You WILL be when you realise just WHO is charging about the countryside looking for you. Anyway, hide behind that barrel and take off your clothes.

JACK   But why?

PUSS   Never mind, for the moment, Master. Just do as I ask. And whatever happens next, do not speak. I will do all the talking for you. Hide, quickly, Master.

PUSS *counts down with* AUDIENCE *10-9-8-7-6-5-4-3-2-1.* KING, WILL, IVAN *and* HUGO *come dashing in right on cue.*

PUSS   Help, help, Your Majesty, my master has been robbed whilst he was bathing. His clothes, money and horse have all been taken.

KING   Good Grief! Where is your master now?

PUSS   He is hiding over there, Your Majesty to hide his... er... his embarrassment! Master... Master...

JACK *rises and comes into view,* IVAN *and* HUGO *move forward as they recognise* JACK.

IVAN   Why it's... *(*PUSS *waves his arm in a spell,* IVAN *and* HUGO *halt and turn)* ...such a cold day to have no clothes on!

KING   Patchett.

HUGO   Yes, Your Majesty?

KING   Go back to the coach, if you can find your way! And get a spare robe for the Marquis, quickly.

HUGO   At once, Your Majesty. *(exits)*

WILL   What cowardly vagabonds would steal a nobleman's possessions? If only I could get my hands on them, they'd know about it.

KING   Quite so, Willie. Considering the Marquis and I are neighbours, we will have to get our heads together to try and stamp out all this crime. What do you say, Marquis?

JACK *looks astonished.*

PUSS   Forgive my master, Your Highness, he is suffering from severe shock just now. *(JACK nods vigorously.)* I am sure you understand. He will recover shortly no doubt. *(JACK shakes his head equally vigorously.)*

KING   Oh, I quite understand. Must have been a ghastly experience. We will take you back to your castle.

JACK *looks horrified. HUGO returns with robe.*
PUSS *takes robe to JACK who can now come fully into view.*

PUSS   *(to JACK)* Go with the King, Master. I will give instructions to the coachman and make all the preparations. Once again, do not appear surprised by anything that happens and try to keep the conversation simple. Tell him you've banged your head or something, I'll run on ahead. *(to KING)* Your offer is most gracious, Your Majesty, my master will be delighted to have you take him to his castle. You will remember that he is not fully recovered, and cannot say a great deal?

KING   Of course. We will take good care of him.

PUSS   Thank you, Sire. I will give your coachman directions and will run on ahead to have everything ready for your arrival. Good day, Your Majesty, Master.

PUSS bows and exits.

KING   Your attendant is extremely efficient, Marquis.

JACK   Yes, he is, Your Majesty. I just don't know what I would do without him. He is most... unusual.

KING   You are quite right. I've never seen an attendant like him before. Ink and Blotchett!

IVAN and HUGO jump to attention.

IVAN)
HUGO)   Yes, Sire?

KING   Hurry on to the palace, explain what has happened and tell them that I shall probably be late for dinner.

HUGO   Yes, Sire. *(stays)*

KING   Are you ready, Marquis? We will make haste to your castle. Willie!

WILL takes JACK'S arm and leads him off after KING. IVAN and HUGO bow.

IVAN   I've got that feeling I should never have got up this morning. Not long ago everything was nice and peaceful around here. Now it's like a madhouse.

DEMON *enters front left.*

DEMON Ha Ha!

HUGO Talk about madhouse it looks like Animal House.

DEMON Now, my faithful partners in crime. I recall that our earlier 'agreement' is now due for its payout! I will take the boots.

HUGO *(to* IVAN*)* Er... He'll take the boots...

IVAN *(to* HUGO*)* He won't, you know.

HUGO *(to* DEMON*)* You won't, you know.

DEMON What?

HUGO *(to* IVAN*)* What?

IVAN I said...

DEMON Are you trying to tell me that you haven't got the boots?

HUGO *(to* IVAN*)* Is that what we are trying to tell him?

IVAN *(to* HUGO*)* What else can we tell him?

HUGO *(to* DEMON*)* Wouldn't you like my shoes instead? They'll be nearer to your size.

DEMON *(enraged)* YOU HAPLESS IDIOTS... YOU INCOMPETENT FOOLS... YOU ARE TOTALLY USELESS... YOU HAVE FAILED IN YOUR TASK. I TOLD YOU IF YOU FAILED, YOU WOULD BE TURNED TO STONE. PREPARE YOURSELVES.

HUGO *gulps.*

IVAN *(to HUGO)* Hey, here's that fiver I owe you.

DEMON Very well...

DEMON *strikes up pose and* FAIRY *comes dashing in and skids to a halt, panting.*

FAIRY Hold it!

DEMON Oh no, not you again!

FAIRY I got here in the nick of time.
To save these two lads in their prime.
You won't succeed with this hideous crime
While The Good Fairy is on Patrol.

DEMON You are too late, aged Fairy dear. These two are to be turned into stone.

FAIRY Hang on to my wand.

IVAN *and* HUGO *hang on to the wand, terrified.*

DEMON *(waving his arms around manically)*
Spirits down in Hades, come.
Evil, badness, darkness run
round this place, this earthly zone
And make these people turn to STONE!

He stops abruptly and freezes in exaggerated posture. The fairy wand has rebounded his spell.

HUGO What's happened?

FAIRY	Do not worry my earthly friends.
We've taken care of his intents.
My wand's too strong, his magic's spent.
Now, he's the one turned to stone.

Come on now lads, let's make him pay.
We'll turn him on his heels one day.
Help me give him a shock today.
I think he deserves it. |

They turn him round and bend him over towards the exit.

HUGO	What are you going to do now?
FAIRY	Just watch.

Now then Demon you're at our mercy.
You do look such a stupid Percy.
No need to bow, parade or curtsy.
Let's send him on his way.
(goes to take a run up, to AUDIENCE*)* Shall I?
Can't hear you. SHALL I? |
| AUDIENCE | YES!! |

FAIRY *kicks him up the rear and sends him flying off stage.*

HUGO	Oh, thank you very much.
IVAN	Yes, you definitely saved our bacon.
FAIRY	Well, with the price of bacon these days, it's worth saving. It's all part of the service. Now try and keep out of his way.
IVAN)
HUGO)	Oh yes, we will etc.

FAIRY   Right, I've to go now. I'm standing in for my friend the Fairy Godmother at [Leeds] as well as looking after you lot. She's gone off sick... and Cinderella's got to go to the ball soon. I'll be back when I'm needed. Bye for now.

FAIRY *exits.*

IVAN   Come on, Hugo, let's get back to the palace before we meet old Hairy Face again.

IVAN *and* HUGO *exit.*
STEW *and* DAME *enter in brownie/scout uniforms with rucksacks, map, magnifying glasses etc.*

STEW   HELLO, FOLKS.

AUDIENCE   HELLO, STEW.

DAME   I'm sure they came this way. *(looks on ground with magnifying glass)*

STEW   *(very bored)* But why are we following everyone else who is following Puss?

DAME   Well, we don't want to miss out on any of the action do we? There's little enough goes on in [Halifax].

STEW   Yes, I suppose so. But where are we now? I think we're lost.

DAME   That's just your trouble... you think too much. Look, I'll show you exactly where we are. *(gets map out and holds it upside down)* We set off down Crooked Hollow... there, turned right at Babbling Brook, across Mushroom Meadow onto

	[Elland Bypass, Huddersfield Road, King Cross Street] (*proudly*) and here we are.

STEW   So, how is it that we're the only ones here?

DAME   We're NOT the only ones here, there's loads of us, LOOK! YOO HOO!

AUDIENCE TYPHOO!!

DAME   They're as daft as we are!

STEW   This place gives me the heeby-jeebies. It's spooky, isn't it?

DAME   Yes, it is. I'm getting the creepy-crawlies. Let's look around to make sure there's no-one here.

They back round opposite sides of the stage and bump into each other centre back, and freeze.

STEW   I knew it. There's something else here, isn't there boys and girls?

AUDIENCE NO.

BOTH   OH YES, THERE IS.

AUD   OH NO, THERE ISN'T.

BOTH   OH YES, THERE IS.

AUDIENCE OH NO, THERE ISN'T.

They slowly turn.

BOTH   OH, IT'S YOU!!

STEW	Well, it's a relief to know the only spook around here is you. Tell you what, let's sing a song with our friends before we go.
DAME	Good idea.

Song 13: I LOVE TO GO A-WANDERING
DAME and STEW with AUDIENCE

STEW	Come on, let's carry on tracking. See you later, folks. BYE, BYE.

They go to exit looking through magnifying glasses.

Curtain.

END OF SCENE ONE

ACT TWO
Scene Two
A forest glade

Curtain set.

Enter PRINCESS *and* QUEEN.

PRINCESS   I'm getting rather worried about father now. They must have been following that cat for hours.

QUEEN   Quite so. Why is it that men always turn little jobs into big ones? They had better find the Marquis of Carabas. He sounds like the ideal husband for you.

PRINCESS   Oh, Mother, I do wish you wouldn't keep trying to match me up with potential husbands, most of them are really quite unsuitable. I will know when I meet the right man. In fact, I am quite attracted to one of the villagers... Jack Dumpling.

QUEEN   What? You couldn't possibly marry a commoner, Annabel... especially one who's name is Dumpling. Can you imagine your introduction at the Lord Mayor's Ball? No, certainly not. But now, 'the Marchioness of Carabas'. That certainly has a ring to it. And he must be quite rich.

PRINCESS   But Mother... money isn't everything. You do want me to be happy don't you?

QUEEN   Of course I do, but there is happy and there is HAPPY. You have a position to uphold when you are a Royal. Now put away these silly notions about this Jack Dumpling. The Marquis of

	Carabas is certainly going to some lengths to impress us.
PRINCESS	He is probably old and fat. The last one you introduced me to had legs like matchsticks... and even those sticks didn't match. His get-up-and-go had got-up-and-gone.
QUEEN	Yes, that was a little unfortunate. But never mind I'm sure the Marquis of Carabas will be a much better choice! Now, don't stop out here too long. I'm going to see if there's any sign of your father coming back. When he does, he'll have to eat a cold dinner... and do the washing up.

QUEEN *exits.*

PRINCESS	It just doesn't seem fair. Sometimes, being a princess is very hard work, and you don't always get what you want. Oh, well, I suppose I'd better try and cheer up a bit.

**Song 14: YOU DON'T ALWAYS GET WHAT YOU WANT
PRINCESS with CHORUS and DANCERS**

PRINCESS *exits.* DEMON *enters.*

DEMON	*(draws boos)* Oh, be quiet you inveterate bunch of hooligans! It's high time I had some success with my plans... and since I can't rely on humans to help... I'll have to do it myself. And I have found the very plan to win my battle with that doddering fairy. Ha Ha Ha! You will see that being nasty is very profitable... and very enjoyable. Ha! I hear someone approaching.

PUSS *enters, sees* DEMON *and stops, warily.*

DEMON	So! Tis my 'friend' the Cat. This is my opportunity! Well, well, well, your arrival is most timely.
PUSS	And what do you mean by that, Mr Demon?
DEMON	I mean it is time that your travels were cur'tailed' somewhat. Ha Ha Ha! Cur'tailed'. Ha Ha… Oh, please yourselves. You have had an easy time so far. But that is now going to stop.
PUSS	And what do you intend to do?
DEMON	I 'intend' to relieve you of your magic boots. That will stop your little schemes.
PUSS	I'm afraid that I am far too busy to join in your little games. I am on my way to the ogre's castle.
DEMON	You are going to the ogre's castle? 'Purr'fect. That will save me a job. There you will meet your match. The ogre is an ogre with magical powers. He'll make mincemeat out of you in no time.
PUSS	I also have magical powers at least as strong as his. I expect a hard contest… but I also expect to win. Nothing will stand in the way of fairness and truth.
DEMON	Bah! Your confidence is to be admired, but you can never live up to it. You will not even get past the ogre's guard. If you go to that castle, it will be the last thing you ever do.
PUSS	We shall see.

DEMON   Why yes, we certainly will see. Ha Ha Ha Ha! Now things are going to work in my favour. That will be the end of Puss in Boots!! Ha Ha Ha Ha!

Draws boos from AUDIENCE *and exits.*

PUSS   The Demon is right. This is the most difficult part of what I have to do… but I have to meet the challenge. And so to the ogre's castle.

Lights dim. PUSS *stays on stage, curtains open on ogre's castle.*

END OF SCENE TWO

ACT TWO
Scene Three
The ogre's castle

OPENING MUSIC FROM "PHANTOM"

Stage is set with OGRE'S *scenery and props, dimly lit.* PUSS *moves upstage.* OGRE'S *voice is amplified from offstage. Suitable shadowy FX.*

OGRE   Fee Fi Fo Fum!
I smell the blood of an Englishman.
Be he alive or be he dead,
I'll grind his bones to make my bread.

Who is it that dares to enter the ogre's castle?

PUSS   It is the Puss in Boots.

OGRE   A Puss in Boots? You have a nerve to invade my privacy, if you do not leave at once, you will make a tasty morsel for my table.

PUSS   I wish to see you, Oh Great One. I have something to discuss.

OGRE   You are an impertinent creature. I have no time to hold discussions with a cat. Methinks you need some encouragement to disappear from my castle... OR ELSE! My guard will soon see you on your way. Come, Dragon and rid the castle of this uninvited guest.

DRAGON *appears and after situation 'fight'* PUSS *wins and* DRAGON *exits.*

OGRE   So! One success to you. Very commendable. But you will get no further. My henchman the Demon Wolf will deal with you.

PUSS   I have already met your Demon Wolf. Bring him out, Great One. I am ready.

OGRE   You are indeed a courageous animal. However, courage alone will not equip you for this. Come Demon!

DEMON *enters to appropriate effects.*

DEMON   So! We meet again… but this time I shall complete my plan… and you will be no more.

FAIRY *enters.*

FAIRY   Just in the nick of time I see.
              I time my entrance perfectly.
              Now, you will have to take on Puss and me,
              Your task will be much harder.

DEMON   Ha! You think that the two of you are a match for me… after one lucky spell? Well, this time you will both be defeated… Ha Ha! Two 'birds' with one stone. Take that!

Space sounds as DEMON *shoots imaginary missiles from his hands.* FAIRY *fends off with her wand. Plenty of effects and strategy.*

FAIRY   It's not as easy as first you thought.
              It's time to finish you off, as I ought.
              That brand-new spell-book that I've just bought
              Has been worth every penny.

DEMON I have more tricks up my sleeve 'dear Fairy'.
Your confidence is misplaced. This is the end for you two!!

Further effects and strategy.

FAIRY Now, it's my turn, you Demon foe.
To command my spirits, no more you'll go
To harm the people in this show.
Your end is well in sight.

All power of goodness, truth and light
Gather behind me for this fight
And stop the Demon with all your might.
(waves wand and DEMON *falls)*
My goodness, Puss, it's worked!
(gazes admiringly at her wand)

Let's remove this pitiful bag of bones.
No more will we hear his dulcet tones.
I could just do now with a pint of Stones.
Let's move this pile of rubbish.

FAIRY *and* PUSS *drag him offstage.*

FAIRY I must leave you now to complete your task.
The powers of good will help if you ask.
I must go and put on my facial mask
With my wrinkles. I buy it by the cask.
(realises that it rhymes, thumps the air, does a dance etc.)

PUSS Thank you, kind fairy. I must do this myself.

FAIRY *waves a spell with her hand and exits.*

OGRE   Fee Fi Fo Fum!
        I STILL smell the blood of an Englishman.

OGRE *footsteps are heard approaching and huge legs appear under ogre's table. Spotlight picks up stage corner with table partly off stage. Stage crew are in wings with ogre's head.*

OGRE   You have done well... so far. My generosity will extend to hearing what you have to say... but you will not leave this castle alive. What is it that brings a puny little cat to see me?

PUSS   Oh Great One, I have heard many stories of your greatness and your magical powers.

OGRE   *(flattered)* You have? And do these stories not frighten you?

PUSS   Oh no, Your Eminence. I am not afraid. My curiosity made me come to see if these stories were true.

OGRE   Have you not heard the story of curiosity killing the cat?

PUSS   Well, yes, I have, but don't forget cats have nine lives.

OGRE   That is true. I must say that you are very brave coming into my castle just out of curiosity.

PUSS   Well, I'm sure some of the tales about you being nasty and wicked are not true. I think you must be lonely living up here on your own.

OGRE   Well, I admit I do get lonely at times... but something usually turns up to relieve my boredom *(Head leans over.)*... like the occasional visitor. *(PUSS backs away.)*

PUSS I have heard many stories of your magical powers. I would like to see some of your magic. Do you think that would be possible?

OGRE I don't see why not. *(Head moves back offstage.)*

Magic trick using stage effects.

PUSS That was marvellous. I've heard that you can change yourself into an animal. Do let me see.

OGRE *(Head leans over.)* You are indeed a fascinated audience, aren't you? Very well, then *(Head moves back and legs disappear.)* I must admit I quite enjoy doing these tricks. Are you ready?

PUSS Yes.

Stage and sound effects of lion (in strobe?) scare PUSS, lion disappears, legs reappear.

OGRE There you are. That gave you quite a fright didn't it?

PUSS *(smoothing down fur)* I was startled for a moment. You did that very well. I'm impressed.

OGRE You are very kind.

PUSS I suppose it's quite easy for you to change into something large. I bet it's difficult... even for you... to change yourself into something small, like a mouse. I bet you can't do that, can you?

OGRE   That's just as easy for me... *(Legs disappear.)* Just watch this.

Stage effect of mouse (in strobe?) PUSS chases round stage, catches mouse and eats it. Big roar that fades away to a squeak.

PUSS   It worked! That's the end of the ogre. *(cheers)* That took a bit longer than I expected. My guests will be here soon. *(looks around)* It's not a bad place. A bit of magic to give it a face lift and it will do nicely.

PUSS waves arm, lights come up, CHORUS and DANCERS appear with feather dusters. Ogre's table disappears.

PUSS   Home sweet Home.

Song 15: IF MY FRIENDS COULD SEE ME NOW
PUSS and CHORUS

Bell/gong, FX.

PUSS   Ah, they have arrived. We could do with a servant or two *(waves arm, maid appears and ushers in MARQUIS, KING and WILL and exits)* Good day, Sire, Master. *(bows)* Are you feeling better?

JACK   *(looking around bemused)* Why yes, the King has been most kind.

PUSS   Thank you, Your Majesty. Please excuse us as we go to my master's dressing room.

KING   Of course.

Bows, PUSS and JACK exit for quick change.

WILL	This is a super castle, Your Majesty. I think the Marquis is going to be quite a catch.
KING	You mean fit for a Princess, Willie? That's just what I was thinking. He's good looking, rich what more could anyone ask for... and he's pleasant into the bargain. We'll have to invite him to a ball at the palace and introduce him to the Princess.
WILL	What a good idea, we haven't had a good knees-up for absolutely ages. The last time was when old Granny Evans went sliding down the banisters and knocked over three servants. It was like a bowling alley. There she was crawling around on her hands and knees...
KING	What did she say to the head chef?
WILL	She said, "Come out from under that table and dance with me."
KING	*(walks around the stage, impressed with the surroundings)* This is a very impressive castle. It has many similarities to the royal palace itself. I'm surprised that it took so long for us to visit this place.
WILL	Perhaps in view of your position in the country, your majesty, the Marquis preferred a more subtle approach... even to make us curious
KING	Well, he certainly succeeded in doing that!

JACK *and* PUSS *enter.*

JACK   Sorry to have kept you waiting, Your Majesty.

KING   Think nothing of it. We have had the opportunity to think of a good way to welcome you into our neighbourhood. We are going to hold a ball at the palace in your honour. You will come, won't you? Then you can meet my… er… subjects and household.

JACK   Yes, of course I will come, thank you.

KING   Wonderful! You make all the arrangements Willie.

WILL   Certainly, Sire. It will be a pleasure.

KING   Right, let's be on our way. We will send your official invitation shortly. Bye for now.

JACK   Goodbye, Your Majesty *(bows)* and thank you for all your help.

Exit KING *and* WILL.

JACK   You really are a wizard Puss. When you were promising all those things, I didn't really think it would all come true. It's just too wonderful for words. Now we can live in grand style and Mother will have no more worries. Now perhaps I will be able to meet Princess Annabel again. How can I ever repay you?

PUSS   I am repaid already by your happiness, Master. I presume I will have a home here myself?

JACK   Of course you will, and you can have anything you wish. I will always be grateful to you for everything.

Song 16: HAPPY NOW FOR EVER MORE
JACK and PUSS

END OF SCENE THREE

ACT TWO
Scene Four
Dame Dumpling's boudoir

Curtain set (boudoir inset, palace ballroom set behind).

Enter STEW, IVAN *and* HUGO.

STEW   HELLO, FOLKS.

AUDIENCE   HELLO, STEW.

STEW   Have you nodded off? HELLO, FOLKS.

AUDIENCE   HELLO, STEW.

STEW   That's amazeballs.

HUGO   Isn't it good now that everyone's troubles have been sorted out.

STEW   It certainly is. And now I'm the Marquis of Carabas's brother. Is that posh or what? I could go and live in [Skircoat] now. It's posh there you know... they've got bidets!

HUGO   Your mother is happy as well now that she's not going to be evicted from her cottage.

STEW   That's right.

HUGO   Tell you what... while you're here, will you help me? I need a bucket of water.

STEW   Yes, alright. We'll help.

HUGO   Oh, thanks.

HUGO *gets bucket from wings.*

STEW   What does he need a bucket of water for?

IVAN   Don't ask me. The other day he went for a dope test. They found out he was one!

HUGO *returns and places empty bucket centre stage, goes to other wings and brings back a cup of water and pours it into bucket.*

IVAN   It's going to take ages to fill it with that.

HUGO   That's why I need your help. *(exits again)*

STEW   Come on, let's see if we can find something bigger.

The three quickly exit and enter from various sides with various receptacles and visibly pour water into the bucket.

HUGO   *(enters finally with another bucket which contains cellophane)* Oh, we've got enough. There isn't room for this now. What shall I do with it?

IVAN   You might as well throw it away.

HUGO   Where shall I throw it?

STEW   *(quietly)* Throw it out there. *(indicates AUDIENCE)*

HUGO   *(quietly)* I can't throw it out there.

STEW/IVAN   OH YES, YOU CAN.

AUDIENCE   OH NO, YOU CAN'T.

STEW/IVAN   OH YES, YOU CAN.

AUDIENCE   OH NO, YOU CAN'T.

HUGO   I can? OK then.

HUGO *does a big spin round and throws cellophane at* AUDIENCE.

STEW   Ha ha ha! Fooled you. See you later.

They exit, taking buckets. Curtain opens on boudoir. DAME *is sploshing around singing Oh, what a beautiful morning, business with props etc., then she notices* AUDIENCE.

DAME   Oh, hello. Isn't it a wonderful day? I feel like dancing the fandango... with a fan in one hand and a dango in the other. Our Jack said everything would work out... and it has. Our Jack's clever, our Jack is. Now he's the Marquis of Carabas... whatever that is! It sounds like a bar of chocolate to me.
And *(looks around confidentially)* we've all got invitations to the royal palace for a ball. Woooh! Is that High Society? I've never had an invitation anywhere before... so I'm making a special effort. Well, when you get to our age, girls. *(peers at* AUDIENCE*)* Oh alright, when you get to my age... it takes a little longer to look young and beautiful.

Song 17: KEEP YOUNG AND BEAUTIFUL
DAME

During song, curtains close to remove inset.

DAME   Oh thank you, thank you, you are wonderful. It's nice to meet an audience who appreciate talent. Well, I have to carry on getting ready. There may be some spare men at the ball… and I'm gonna knock 'em dead. Well, that's what usually happens! See you later, bye bye.

DAME *exits.*

END OF SCENE FOUR

ACT TWO
Scene Five
The royal ballroom

Dance 18:
CHORUS and DANCERS

Applause as dance ends. Music starts up again quietly. WILL *announces from rostrum.*

WILL	Ladies and Gentlemen, pray silence for his Majesty's guests: Baron Stewart Dumpling, Lord Ivan Itch and Sir Hugo Crotchett. *(bows and curtsies)*
HUGO	*(to* WILL*)* Scratchett!!
WILL	I beg your pardon?
HUGO	Sir Hugo Scratchett.
WILL	Oh, sorry. Silly me. *(slaps own hand)*

STEW, IVAN *and* HUGO *acknowledge* CHORUS *and move to front.*

STEW	This is marvellous, isn't it. I always knew Jack had a bright future, but I never thought we'd end up as wealthy landowners. My friends will be green with envy.
IVAN	And I never thought I'd ever be invited to a royal ball.
HUGO	I could get quite used to this Sir Hugo business. It's got quite a ring to it.

STEW   Yes, rather like a diving bell! Ha Ha!

IVAN   Shall we join in the dancing?

HUGO   Oh yes, lets.

STEW   Come on then.

They select three girls. IVAN *picks one near front of stage.* STEW *and* HUGO *watch.*

IVAN   Excuse me.

GIRL   Yes.

IVAN   That's the answer, now for the question.

GIRL   What do you mean?

IVAN   Will you dance with me?

GIRL   Of course.

They start dancing.

STEW   I think I'll have a go (*he kneels in front of* GIRL 2) Excuse me, may I dance with you?

GIRL 2   Certainly not. Do you think I'm going to dance with a child?

STEW   Oh, pardon me. *(gets up)* I didn't know you were expecting. *(He dances with another girl.)*

HUGO   Could I have the pleasure of this dance?

GIRL 3   I don't usually dance with perfect strangers.

HUGO   Who's perfect? *(they dance)*

WILL *comes to rostrum, music stops.*

WILL   My Lords, Ladies and Gentlemen, pray silence for King Basil, Queen Sybil and Princess Annabel.

ALL *bow and curtsy, music starts again.*

KING   It's quite nice to have another ball... and maybe we'll have something to celebrate.

PRINCESS   Father!

QUEEN   Now, I do hope you are going to be on your best behaviour this evening, Basil.

KING   Yes, Sybil dear.

QUEEN   I do hope you won't have too much wine and try the Lambada again.

KING   No, my precious.

WILL *goes to the rostrum again.*

WILL   Your Royal Highnesses, my Lords, Ladies and Gentlemen, pray silence for His Majesty's guest... Dame Dumpling.

DAME *enters to some upmarket hazy music, dressed in totally way out gear to great effect. She moves to royals. Music starts again quietly. Big curtsy.*

DAME   Good evening, Basil. So naice to see you hagain.

QUEEN	Do you know this... this... lady?
KING	Only a passing acquaintance, my dear.
DAME	Nearly so. You almost evicted me from my cottage.
QUEEN	Oh, I'm sure it must have been a clerical error. Isn't that right, Basil?
KING	Yes, my dear.
DAME	How about a dance, Your Maj?

WILL *moves to rostrum.*

WILL	Your Royal Highnesses, my Lords, Ladies and Gentlemen...
KING	Saved by the bell!!
WILL	Pray silence for his Majesty's guest, the Marquis of Carabas.

Bows and curtsies, music starts.

KING	There you are Marquis, so nice to see you again. Are you now fully recovered?
JACK	Yes, thank you Your Majesty. I have never felt better... and may I say what a lovely palace you have.
KING	You are very gracious. Let me introduce you to my wife, Queen Sybil.

JACK	*(bows)* It is an honour to meet you, Your Highness.
QUEEN	Thank you, Marquis.
KING	And allow me to introduce you to my daughter, Princess Annabel.

Bow and curtsy, KING *and* QUEEN *move away.*

PRINCESS	You look very smart, Marquis. In fact, you look familiar. You made my heart flutter a little.
JACK	And you look like the girl of my dreams. I have been waiting such a long time to meet you.
PRINCESS	You are very kind, Marquis.
JACK	Call me Jack, Your Highness.
PRINCESS	Then you must call me Annabel.
JACK	May I have this dance, Annabel.
PRINCESS	Of course.
KING	Don't they look lovely together?
QUEEN	Yes, they do.
DAME	They look so nice, I think I'm going to cry.
QUEEN	Basil, hankie!
KING	Yes, my precious *(passes hankie to* DAME*)*
DAME	*(blows her nose loudly)*

KING	Your son is a very fine young man.
DAME	Why, thank you. *(blows her nose again)*

**Dance 19: TRULY MADLY DEEPLY
JACK and PRINCESS**

ALL OTHERS *continue dancing,* PRINCESS *and* JACK *move to* KING, QUEEN *and* DAME.

PRINCESS	Mother, Father... I realise that this may come as a shock to you... but the Marquis wishes to ask you something.
KING	Oh yes, what is it my boy?
JACK	Well, I know that I have only met your daughter this evening, but *(they look at each other)* we feel we have known each other for ages. I would like to ask you formally for Princess Annabel's hand in marriage.
DAME	WHOOPEE!... oh... er... sorry.
KING	Yes, of course you can.

Rousing cheer.

PRINCESS	*(hugs* KING *and* QUEEN*)* Oh, thank you. I'm the happiest girl in the whole world. *(hugs* JACK*)*
KING	Willie.
WILL	Yes, I know, Sire. I will make all the arrangements.

Song 20: SUPERCALIFRAGILISTICEXPIALIDOCIOUS
FULL CAST and CHORUS

After song, big cheer and curtain.

STEW, IVAN and HUGO walk through the curtain for the community song.

STEW	Hello Folks!
AUDIENCE	Hello Stew!
STEW	Oh Come on, you can do better than that – HELLO FOLKS!
AUDIENCE	HELLO STEW!
DAME	That's much better! Have you enjoyed yourselves?
AUDIENCE	YES!!
IVAN	That's brilliant! Isn't that brilliant, Hugo?
HUGO	It certainly is! It's brilliant, Ivan.
DAME	It could be even more brilliant tomorrow!!
STEW	Well now it's time for you to do some work. It's sing-a-long time. Are you ready?
AUDIENCE	(Not sure) Y-y-y yes.
IVAN	Come on – ARE YOU READY?
HUGO	OH NO YOU'RE NOT!

AUDIENCE   OH YES WE ARE!!

DAME   Let's do it while they're ready.

STEW   Let's do it while they're still here.

They sing it through. They try with audience, but they need some words. DAME *pulls out a small piece of paper.*

DAME   There you are.

AUDIENCE   "Can't read them"/ "They're too small."

DAME   They need some bigger words.

Either words are dropped from the flies, or IVAN *and* HUGO *go to fetch a word board. They all sing together, then audience is split into two sides which sing against each other with* DAME *and* STEW *each 'conducting' a side ("We were better than you", "Oh, no you weren't." Eventually call it a draw).*

DAME   Right, we'll call it a draw. I'm off to get ready for the wedding. Why don't you sing it one more time now they're really warmed up? See you soon – Bye-eee!

DAME *exits for costume change. They sing the song through once more and all exit waving. Dancers do a short piece, ending with their bows and splitting to the sides of the stage as the walkdown begins.*

WALKDOWN

Song 21   THE BEST OF TIMES IS NOW (music only)

DANCERS

CHORUS

DEMON

FAIRY

KING and QUEEN

STEWART DUMPLING

IVAN and HUGO

DAME DUMPLING

WILL

PRINCESS ANNABEL and JACK

PUSS IN BOOTS

Usual rhyme ending

FINALE SONG AND CURTAIN

THE END

Props and Sound Effects

PROLOGUE
magic wand for fairy (needed for every appearance)

ACT ONE
Scene One
- skateboard or scooter
- hankie
- foghorn effect
- percussion effects

Scene Two
- coffee trolley, with cups, water spray, hammer, flaps (one flap at head height opening for the prop hammer and one at shin height to hit actor's posterior as it opens). The trolley should be built on wheels so that the 'operator' inside it can be wheeled on and off.
- coins
- letter

Scene Three
- bottle of pills
- sack of bran
- box (to catch rabbit in)
- red boots
- rabbit
- Yorkshire Post
- big glasses

Scene Five
> throne(s)
> dead grouse
> swannee whistle

ACT TWO

Scene One
> barrel (to hide behind)
> spare robe (for Jack)
> five Pound note
> 2 rucksacks
> map
> 2 magnifying glasses

Scene Three
> ogre's head and legs
> ogre's table

Scene Four
> 2 buckets, one with cellophane
> water
> cup and other small containers to carry it in
> boudoir props for Dame

Scene Five
> rostrum
> hankie
> foghorn effect

NOTES

NOTES

www.ingramcontent.com/pod-product-compliance
Lightning Source LLC
Chambersburg PA
CBHW071728040426
42446CB00011B/2262